The subject matter vocabulary have been selected with expert assistance, and the brief and simple text is printed in large, clear type.

Children's questions are anticipated and facts presented in a logical sequence. Where possible, the books show what happened in the past and what is relevant today.

Special artwork has been commissioned to set a standard rarely seen in books for this reading age and at this price.

Full-colour illustrations are on all 48 pages to give maximum impact and provide the extra enrichment that is the aim of all Ladybird Leaders.

Index of Contents

A Ladybird Leader
sounds

written by Allan P. Sanday
illustrated by Bernard H. Robinson

Publishers: Ladybird Books Ltd . Loughborough
© Ladybird Books Ltd 1975
Printed in England

Sounds in the street

What sounds do we hear in the street?
Think how many different ones there are.
We hear the engines of cars, buses,
motor cycles and trucks.

4

We hear horns, brakes, gears
and car doors shutting.

We hear people's voices and footsteps.

What is the noisiest thing in this picture?

Sounds in the country

The countryside is full of sounds.
You can still hear engines
of different sorts.
But other sounds are more interesting

If you listen carefully you can hear
many kinds of bird song,
the sounds of animals
and the wind in the trees.

Sounds in the home

Home is a noisy place
now electricity is used there.

There are many sounds
people did not hear 100 years ago.

We can hear a vacuum cleaner,
a washing machine, a radio,
a television, a hair-dryer
and even an electric drill.

9

What is sound?

If some grains of rice
are put on a drum
and the drum is banged,
they will jump up and down
as the drum 'vibrates'.
Sound is caused when things vibrate.

A violin string will vibrate
if a bow is pulled across it.
When it vibrates we hear a sound.

Wrap tissue paper round a comb.
Put your lips against it and hum.
Can you feel the paper vibrate
as you make the sound?

13

Sound from your voice-box

Put your hand gently against your throat and say a long, 'Ah'.

Can you feel the vibrations in your voice-box?

A simple telephone

Thread a long string between two
plastic cartons.

Hold one carton and let your friend
hold the other. Keep the string taut.

When you speak into your carton,
your friend can hear you in his.

The vibrations pass along the string.

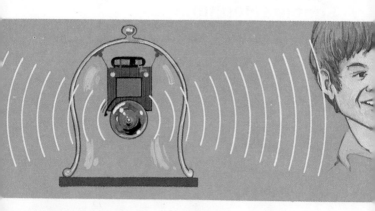

When the electric bell rings
inside the 'bell-jar', we can hear it.

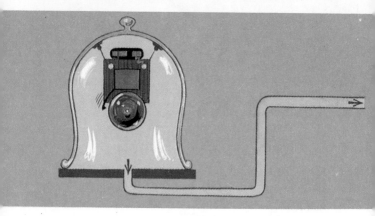

If all the air is pumped out of the jar,
we cannot hear the bell.

So sound travels through air.

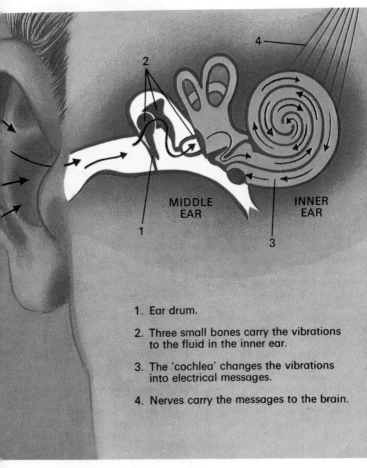

MIDDLE
EAR

INNER
EAR

1. Ear drum.

2. Three small bones carry the vibrations
   to the fluid in the inner ear.

3. The 'cochlea' changes the vibrations
   into electrical messages.

4. Nerves carry the messages to the brain.

Sound travels through the air
to our ears.

Then it makes the ear drum vibrate
and we hear the sound.

Sound can travel through the groun

This Indian tracker is listening
for the sound of horses' hooves.

Sound travels along metal
and through water.

Here are two experiments for you to try.

Another experiment

Sound travels through the air
which is in the hose pipe.

The speed of sound

'e see lightning before we hear thunder
though they happen at the same time.

ght travels faster than sound.

ound travels through air at 330 metres
r second (about 739 miles an hour).

Some sounds are quiet —

The ticking of a watch is a quiet sound.

An explosion is a very loud sound.

Sounds can be made louder

The wooden part of a cello
is like an empty box.

When the cello string vibrates,
this 'sound-box' makes the sound loude

Making voices louder

We can make our voices louder
by speaking through a megaphone.

Try making a megaphone
with a cone of paper.

Very loud sounds

The sounds of pop groups
are amplified (made very loud).
Listening to very loud sounds
can harm your ears.

Sounds can be made quieter

The tiles on this classroom ceiling absorb (take in) some of the sound.

Not all tiles can do this.

These are special tiles.

Hearing quiet sounds

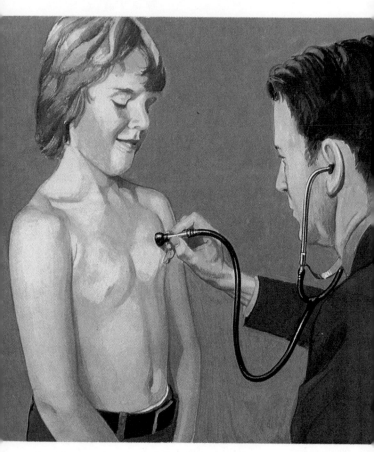

A doctor can listen to the sound
of a heartbeat.

He uses a 'stethoscope',
a special tube for listening.

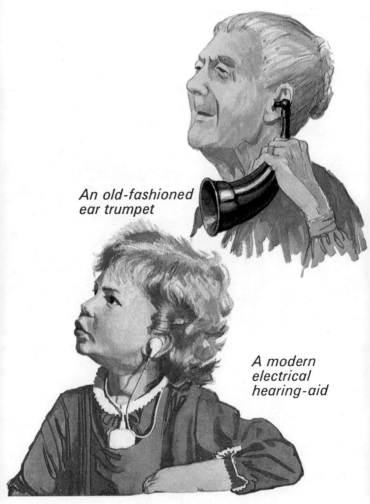

An old-fashioned ear trumpet

A modern electrical hearing-aid

An ear-trumpet is just a tube
for people to speak into.

The modern hearing-aid is smaller
and neater.

High sounds and low sounds

Stand some milk bottles in a row.

Put a different amount of water in eac[h]

Tap the bottles.

Those with little water and much air
make a high sound.

Those with much water and little air
make a low sound.

The sound of a violin string becomes
higher as it is stretched tighter.

The lower sounding strings
are thicker than the higher ones.

The boys have high voices.
The men have lower voices.
All of them can sing loudly or softly.

ome singers can sing a note so high
at it will break a wine glass close by.

ne man is blowing a special dog whistle.
ne sound is too high for a man to hear,
ut the dog can hear it.

33

Echoes

When a sound bounces back,
it is called an 'echo'.

The sound of this horn bounces back
from the side of the mountain.

The whispering gallery
in St. Paul's Cathedral, London

A whisper close to the wall,
can be heard round the other side.

This is because the sound travels
round the wall.

Echoes under water

This ship finds the submarine by echoes

High-pitched sounds travel down
from the ship to the submarine.

They echo back to the ship.

Echoes in the dark

ats make high-pitched squeaks
hen they fly.

e squeaks echo from things in the way.

en the bats can avoid these things.

Sounds have meanings

In the morning, the ringing of the alarm means it is time to get up.

When the whistle blows,
it means the water is boiling.

When the 'pinger' rings,
it means the food is cooked.

Warning sounds

The horn warns that a car is coming.

The siren warns that a fire-engine is coming.

The fog-horn warns that a ship is near.

The burglar-alarm warns if the shop is being robbed.

Understanding sounds

Sounds help us to understand
one another.

Sometimes we cannot understand
the sounds other people make!

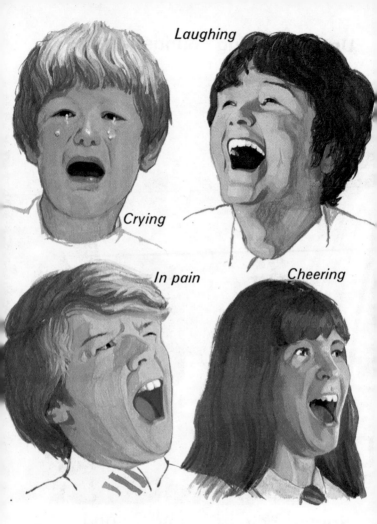

Laughing

Crying

In pain

Cheering

Sounds that show feelings

We know how people feel
when they make these sounds.

Animal sounds

Animals have sounds of their own
to show other animals how they feel.

Sending sounds over long distances

by native drums

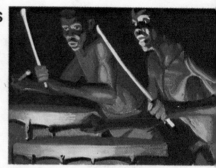

by telephone

by radio

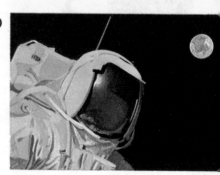

Storing sounds

on records

on tape

Sounds we like

Some sounds can be joined together
to make music.

There are many different kinds of musi

Not all people like the same kind.

Sounds we do not like

When we live near other people
we must be careful
of the sounds we make.

In some factories, the noise is so loud
that the workers must cover their ears.
They cannot hear if anyone speaks
so they have to read each others lips.

Some of us live in quiet places.
Others are not so lucky.
Most of us would not choose
to live near to a busy airport.

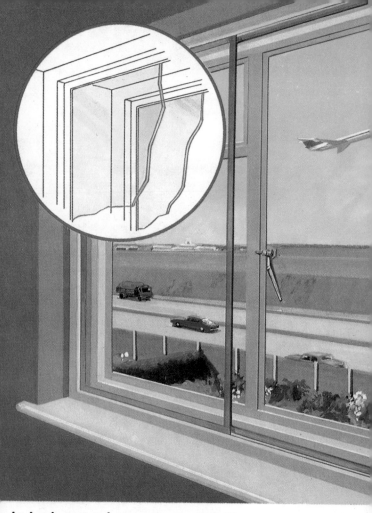

It helps to keep out noise
if windows are double-glazed.

This means there are two sheets of glas
with a space between them.

With so much noise in the world
we have to listen carefully
to the things that are worth hearing.

You can prove that vibrations make sounds

Hold a bell quite still whilst it is sounding.

Its vibrations will 'kick away' a bead on a thread.

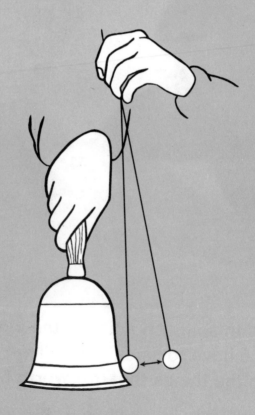